I0625475

The Secrets My Clothes Could Tell

By

Ocelee Tonya Qualls

Contents

Prayer

Preface

Prayer

Dear Heavenly Father I thank you for the content in this book. I thank you for my experiences both good and bad because they molded me into the person you created me to be. I ask that this book will be a blessing and encouragement to all who read it. I ask that those who may be feeling like they are less than, will feel and know that they are of royal priesthood and that they are valuable, valued, loved, and needed. I pray they know they were not a mistake, that you called them into this world to shine their light on others. I declare and decree that they will not allow the opinion of others to dim their light. God guard their hearts and their minds and direct their paths. Reinforce your word and promises in their lives. Increase their faith and knowledge of you and imbed in their DNA that they CAN do all things through Christ who gives them strength. In Jesus name I pray.

~Amen

Preface

The Secrets My Clothes Could Tell is a book about healing. So often we go through life trying to hide our pasts from everyone, even God; however, impossible, especially when the bible tells us in Hebrews 4:13 that *nothing in all creation is hidden from God's sight. Everything is uncovered and laid bare before the eyes of him to whom we must give account.*

No matter where we go there is one thing that holds true… Let's face it, we have all done things in our past of which we are not proud. Some of the things that I have done have not always exemplified the love of Christ and we know that God is love. He also tells us that vengeance is his, but in my humanity I have not always allowed God to oversee it for me. I figured since I was a Scorpio that if someone hurt me or did me wrong, oh I had to sting them and I had to get them good. Some things that I did were openly done and some of it was done in secret. I mean, you should never let the right hand know what the left hand is doing… until now only a select few knew about me taking a couple of my exes' toothbrushes and cleaning the toilet with them. I felt if they were going to talk crap to me, then I was going to give them some crap. I was often the girlfriend that would help all her friends get back at their significant others. There were some things I would let God manage but the minor things I took into my own hands; I knew it was not right, but at the time I did not even think about it. The older I got I realized that I could not pick and choose where or what part of my life I wanted God in, but I had to allow him to be in my life always, leading and guiding me. I am so glad that I have been delivered from pettiness and that get even spirit. But honey, if the clothes on our backs could hear and could talk, what secrets could they tell about us? I bet they are things you would not want anyone to know!!!

"You can't fix what you are not willing to face." –Elisa Haney Sanders

Chapter 1

Who Am I

No matter the obstacles I have faced in life, I never gave up hope or lost my faith. Through the childhood hurt regarding my weight which later turned into adult hurt, the many failed relationships, the frustration of never using my Associate, Bachelor's, or Master's degrees, the disappointments of always being overlooked at work for advancement or promotion, the many so called friends who I was there for when they were going through but when I needed them their lives were way too busy to stop and uplift me, and the most devastating of all events that I had to endure, was the death of my Papa Bear (My wonderful dad) the only earthly man who loved me completely and unconditionally, I never gave up on what I believed. I would bend but not break. This would later become my motto in life which is probably why Isaiah 43:2 is a very prophetic scripture that speaks to my very soul, "*when thou passest through the waters, I will be with thee; and through the rivers, they shall not overflow thee: when thou walkest through the fire, thou salt not be burned; neither shall the flame kindle upon thee.*" I would hear stories about how women would go through various life experiences and how they wanted to give up, but that was never an option for me. Giving up was not and has never been a part of my DNA.

I often questioned why God allowed me to go through the hardships I did, to me it just didn't make sense, especially after having set myself up for success regarding my education, it puzzled me why I never achieved it.

As far as love was concerned I always had a great blueprint of what love was supposed to be by watching my parents. My mother always praying for us and making sure we were active in the church and my father always thought the world of me and told me "No man was ever good enough for me." He always encouraged me and told me that there was nothing I could not do or accomplish. He was a hard-working man, who despite being born with polio, worked all his life to achieve his goals and take care of his family.

Apart from the two womanizers I dated, most of the men I attracted had no drive and no ambition. Not any of these men were even close to the caliber of man my dad was. What then did I see in them, or what was it in me that kept attracting men with no drive, alcohol abusers, drug users, manipulators, and narcissist? I know now that it was part of my process. I would need to go through things to get to where God needed me to be. I remember hearing someone once say that "there was purpose in the pain." That let me know that no matter what the enemy tried to throw my way, no matter what had been taken from me, no matter how many times I had been overlooked, lied on, talked about, that it was not all in vain. The Lord wanted to use my struggles and pain to push me to greater and to help someone along the way. As my spiritual mother, Prophetess Christena Rollins had said to me on numerous occasions, you cannot have a testimony without a test.

My love life was the one area the enemy had always tried to attack me in the most. At least early on that is, because later he would try to hinder and bind up my finances when he saw that no matter what he tried to do by way of a nogood man could ever make me give up on love. I always mustarded up enough love to give to the next person and I never stopped believing in it. Love is the foundation of my very being. The word tells us in 1 Thessalonians 3:12 "*May the Lord make your love increase and overflow for each other*." I just kept replenishing love even when the enemy tried to send men and artificial friends my way to deplete it. I look at it as a Job experience where the Lord allowed the enemy to take his possessions, but not kill him. I believe the Lord gave permission for the enemy to try me in the area of love because the Lord already knew the enemy would not succeed. The Lord knew that my story would serve as an avenue to bring healing to many who have encountered or may encounter hurt of any kind, disappointments, let downs, whose trust has been defiled by someone they thought loved them.

The Secrets My Clothes Could Tell

When God gave me this book to write, for years… (at least 15 years) I toiled over how I wanted to approach it. Was I to approach it from a "tell all" standpoint and expose all involved, or was I to be discrete and write it as if I was telling a story about someone else? This impasse would cause me many years of delayed advancement in getting this assignment completed for the Lord. As smart as I proclaim to be, it sure took me a long while to get things in order. I had prophesies of birthing a book, of God handing me my gift and I kept putting it on the shelf, that God would give me as far as I could see… As far as I could see, It was my daughter's God mother who prophesied that to me when I was twenty-two or so. I was dating a man I had no business dating really; he was older than I was, 13 years to be exact. He came along when God told me he was going to bless me as far as I could see…he cheated on me, he had two children with another woman in the span of a 3-year relationship, I could not see further than him. The enemy is listening to what God has planned for us, so do not think that when God wants or says he is going to bless you that you will not have issues and problems, because with greatness and elevation comes major warfare. The enemy does not want us to complete our purpose that God designed us for. I am so glad to know that with the Lord, I am on the winning team. I would think the devil would be so frustrated with all the losses he has taken concerning me, but he never gives up and neither should we. No matter what I have been through I still love God, I still love people, I still encourage people and I forgive everyone who has ever wronged me.

God graces us with many gifts in different areas. I have always been very compassionate and forgiving, even when it hurt. I had to forgive and love people as if they never did me any harm. It is only by the grace of God that I am able to do this.

Chapter 2

The Childhood hurt

"What you say can preserve life or destroy it" (Proverb, 18:21 *Contemporary English Version*). Childhood hurt can last a lifetime if you allow it to do so. For too long I let the things that were said to me as a child have dominion and power over my life. I knew that words could hurt, but I never knew the magnitude those words could have regarding the various people and the different kinds of spirits I would attract throughout my adulthood.

This was a hard chapter for me to write because no one wants to face the pain of the past; I have often wondered if my classmates knew just how much all their words cut me to my core. Their negative words about me overpowered the positive words my family spoke over me and my life. Their words cut me deep!!! I became self-conscious and I started to second guess myself and feel that people would look at my outer appearance and not see who I was inside. I'm so glad to know that while man looks at our outward appearance, God looks at our hearts.

For years I allowed their untruths to penetrate my foundation, and those mean evil words took root in my life. I was no longer the happy girl who tried to make everyone smile; I became the girl who had to always defend herself and try to walk on eggshells around everyone. I tried to be invisible so others would not talk about me, but it did work out that way, their words just kept digging, hurting, and chipping away at my inner being.

I remember kids calling me fat and huge, no one ever called me ugly though, but their words made me feel ugly.

The Secrets My Clothes Could Tell

Once I overhead a very well-known basketball player say to someone "look at her trying to act skinny." Trying to act skinny... I could not figure out for the life of me how I was trying to act skinny...exactly how does skinny act?

I was simply being myself and yet that was not good enough. I assume he thought I should have been quiet and introverted, but I was happy. God made me happy and no matter how people knowingly or unknowingly tried to tear me down, I am still standing. By the grace of God, I did not lose my mind, but I overcame. It was not easy but with God all things are possible.

As I sit back and self-reflect it floors me how I allowed myself to be identified or defined by demeaning words throughout my prime school years. I even accepted the name people called me in high school "big O." I absolutely despised that name. That name would later cause me to have a serious complex. It would make my skin crawl to hear anyone use the word big in front of me. I would cringe and be so crushed inside when someone used that word in my presence. I did not care if they were talking about a big diamond, if they said big, I died inside. After high school that was the end of all that name calling and taunting right? Incorrect! The hurt spilled over into my adulthood as well. A girlfriend of mine told me a friend of hers wanted to meet me. Personally, I believe she was trying to get rid of him and used me as a way to do it. Nonetheless, she introduced us, and his words to her were, "I like big girls, but she was huge." and once again I found myself being the brunt of someone's cruelty, but not as a child, as an adult. Years later and after losing a substantial amount of weight this same guy saw me and tried to talk to me. I politely declined his advances.

I know this chapter is titled childhood hurt, but I would be remiss if I did not mention a situation that I encountered as an adult that made me feel like I was back in grade school and high school. Imagine being 35, very much an adult, and you meet this very handsome, charming, charismatic, smooth talking man who one day out the blue asks you a question that takes you back to your childhood and adds to the hurt you felt years ago that you thought you had moved past only to find that you had only suppressed it. He asked me how it felt to be the biggest person in my family. At this time in my life, I had lost over 100 pounds. I was feeling really good and confident about myself, and I felt pieces of that confidence being chipped away at every time he would laugh and taunt me as if I was still a child. I never knew that such silliness could follow a person into adulthood. All this was a direct effect of the hole that was dug during my youth, filled with the seed of their malicious words that were planted and took on roots that ran deep. My now self would never have dealt with such an idiot. I do not care how educated he was, he should have never been a part of my life to the extent he was. He saw that self-doubt had been planted years before him and he played on it.

I now can forgive them for all the name calling and the hurtful words and leaving me out of things because they thought I could not do it. I also forgive myself. It took me a long time to appreciate myself and my differences and things that set me apart from others. I now realize that I am fearfully and wonderfully made and that our Heavenly Father makes no mistakes; I am made in his likeness, and he thinks the world of me. So, see it does not matter how others look at me or view me, to God I am royalty, I am his daughter just as the people who caused the offenses are his children. I forgive them because I will not allow the hurt of the past stop me from moving forward into my destiny. For every bad name they called me, I forgive them. For every time they lied on me and had other children following me home to fight me, over something I NEVER said, I forgive them. Forgiveness is something that has always been there, but it feels good to let it be known that all is forgiven and because of my Lord and savior I can love them with the love of God and from a pure place. Healing feels good!

Chapter 3

Forgiveness

Matthew 6:14-15

For if you forgive men their trespasses, your heavenly father will also forgive you. But if you do not forgive men their trespasses, neither will your Father forgive your trespasses.

As long as I can remember I have always been the type of person who never really held a grudge. Believe you me, there were times I wished I could have stayed mad at people, but God would not let me. I used to ask him why he made me so compassionate and caring about other's feelings even though they did not care about mine and it was apparent they did me wrong. I could have a yelling match with a person, and their words and actions could cut me to my core, and it would seem as though an hour or two later, I would totally forget about what they had done. I remember a co-worker whom I used to consider a friend, getting mad at me because I was laughing and talking with my supervisor whom I had gotten into it with. I had to explain to her that God did not wire me to stay mad or harbor any ill feelings towards anyone. I believe that you should kill people with kindness. What we need to realize as children of God is that we need to forgive others because God teaches us to forgive, it releases us from the situation. If we do not forgive we stay bound by that which was only supposed to be momentary. We also run the

risk of our heavenly father not forgiving us, and I don't know about you, but I mess up daily and if God was not gracious and loving enough to forgive me I don't know where I would be.

When you forgive others you gain freedom and liberty. There is healing in forgiveness, deliverance in forgiveness, youthfulness, and long life in forgiveness. I often have people tell me that I look younger now than I did when I was younger. I can attribute that to the fact that I forgive and move on. While I may have seeked vengeance on people in the past and obtained temporary gratification, I found out that when you let go and let God handle the situation you don't have to worry about any backlash or retaliation and you can live free from any guilt that you may have felt from doing something mean and sinister. It also helps when you know who you are in Christ. Let us not forget that our heavenly father loves us, and he has armies to fight for us; we need only relinquish our desires to God and watch him handle it.

Throughout my life I had to forgive many people for a lot of awful things. One time a guy that I had just got done fornicating (do not act like I'm the only one) with looked me dead in my face told me he loved me and knew he had my checkbook in his pocket. Talk about deceit and betrayal. When he left out of my door, he and 2 other people drove to my bank, went in and cashed a check for $501.01… imagine my shock when I got the call as I was at a doctor's appointment, an appointment that would determine whether or not I was mentally fit to have weight loss surgery. I thank God my mental breakdown in that doctor's office did not stop him from approving me for the surgery. By the time this guy and his friends got done with my checkbook, they ended up writing over $4000 worth of bad checks, all over Peoria and its neighboring cities on a closed account. I cannot even write checks at certain places to this day…But I declare and decree that my name is cleared. I will no longer be bound by the scheme of the enemy. I serve a God that is mighty, and he is making my name great and canceling debt caused by these malicious people who let the devil use them.

The enemy is very bold. Even when he knows he has tried to destroy you he will try to come at you from all angles. This guy had the nerve to contact me throughout the years (my cell phone number has been the same for over 20 years), trying to make small talk. He spent time in jail for another offense shortly after he tried to destroy me by writing checks, gassing up cars, and pulling off without paying. I do not believe he ever received punishment from the state for what he did to me. I would run into him at different stores throughout the city. I have a cousin who is close to some of his family members and if I was on the phone talking with her and he came around, he would always try to grab the phone to talk. Each time he would try to talk to me or if he approached me if he saw me out somewhere I would simply say this phrase "*what??? You're not in jail*" and he would end up right back in prison. I often said that was God allowing me to have solace about the situation. It wasn't until I completely healed that I was able to tell this guy that I forgive him, and he was released from having to go back to jail every time I spoke that phrase into the atmosphere. It took a lot of growth and denouncing of soul ties and being set free for me to truly be able to look this man in the face and tell him I forgive him. He had a smirk on his face and even tried asking if he could call me. I just looked at him and said I respectfully decline. I knew that God had worked something out in me when I did not yell aloud in the store for everyone to hide their purses because there was a thief passing through, which I had often done when I would see him out!

I once dated a womanizer. He had a proclivity for alcohol. He would lie and use his good looks to get away with using each woman he encountered. I met this man at a little hole in the wall bar here. I was never one to frequent bars, but I was out with my cousin and decided to go in with her. As I was sitting at the bar minding my own business and laughing at the way those folks were looking in the mirror at themselves and dancing, this man walked up to me. I take that back, his partner walked up to me, and he slid in between us and took over. The first thing he said to me was "you got some beautiful eyes; God bless your mama". I chuckled at his lameness and had I known better I would have run out of the club as if I had gasoline underwear on but I stayed and talked with him a while. He alluded to the fact that he wanted to give me a hug and I told him since I did not know him I would just shake his hand. I, being in Ocelee flirtation mode, got a hair brained idea to go to the store and buy some Hershey hugs… I went back into the club and told him that I wanted to give him a hug now and when he came in for the hug, I put the Hershey hugs in his hand and told him to have a great night. That was a huge mistake, I not only had to hug him for real, but this was the start of another hurtful journey of my life, one that was riddled with deceit and lies. This man introduced me to his family members. His uncle was dating a young lady who had two daughters; I became very close to these two young ladies. Imagine how I felt when two different family members told me he was sleeping with one of them. I did not see it at all. I was just hanging out, having a grand old time and I was being manipulated and deceived. Spending time with them, going places with them and having them over my house not knowing I was being used. The young lady who was sleeping with who I thought was my man at the time would always tell me about her love life, with an old classmate of mine, but what she was doing was describing her intimate moments with the man I was dating. That was a hard pill to swallow, because I take my friendships very seriously and I truly considered her to be a sister and even though it would take years for me to truly face the hurt from this situation, it was a situation I had to find forgiveness in. Forgiveness does not mean that what the person did or said to you was right, but forgiveness means that no matter what they said to you or how they treated you, you refuse to let that hold you back or keep you down.

Another situation that I had encountered while I was dating this guy was when the mother of one of his children had written on my car with eyeliner pencil the words YOU ARE SUCH A LIAR, she let the air out of all my tires and had broken out the back window of my car. Had I not permitted him to use my car and allowed him access into my life these things could have been avoided. Sometimes we must be honest with ourselves and looking back I made some poor choices in my life and through them all God never left my side. He kept having my back. The young lady who flattened my tires, broke my car window, and wrote on my car later ended up in prison with a very good friend of mine and to show you how God works, because I went looking for this girl after she broke my car window, and I could not find her. I then gave the situation to God and asked him to handle it. See at that time I could not understand why all these terrible things were happening to me, but I knew who to call on in time of trouble. As aforementioned, the young lady who tore up my car told my friend to convey to me that she was deeply sorry for what she had done to my car. She knew it was not her ex's car, but she wanted to get back at him. She also stated that ever since she did that to me her life went on a rollercoaster ride. She had started doing drugs and prostituting which landed her in prison, she said she felt like God allowed her to go through things because she knew I was a child of God, and she had no business touching my property. See God will vindicate you. You need only turn the matter over to the father who knows exactly what to do. As my spiritual mom Prophetess Christena always tells me… redemption is for everybody. My prayer is that this young lady lives a long healthy and prosperous life. I pray that God turned her situation around for her and that she has found true love. That jealousy and hurt is uprooted out of her life and that she will know how precious she is in the sight of God. I realize that this man not only hurt me but every woman he dated and lied to. And there were a lot of women he deceived.

I hope I am not getting ready to give away my age by telling you this next story… I met this guy from the state of Washington on the PL and for those of you who do not know, that stands for phone line. It was called a chat line, some called it the party line. It was just something to do while you sat in the house bored. You could call in listen to introductory messages that people would leave about themselves, and you could leave them a message or go into a private conversation with them. This guy and I talked over the phone for some months. Back in the day we used to get some preconceived idea about how a person looked by their voice. I think the phrase we used was "he sounds cute or he sound like he look good", going strictly off of voice because video chat was not even a thing then. We would write each other often and talk all the time. I had sent him pictures of me, but he would never send pictures of himself. That red flag should have gone up but I think my red flag detector was broken. He told me he favored one of the guys in that R & B group Shai, and none of those guys were bad looking so I got this idea of how he looked and then put the nice voice with the thought of how he looked…Houston we have a match, or so I thought. My girlfriends at State farm use to say Oce, what if this guy is butt ugly. I would tell them that he is not but looks aren't important, love is. They would go on for months teasing me about him and how he might look and what if he had one eye, what if his teeth were rotten, I mean my girls went in hard, but I just stuck to the fact that this man's voice was nice and he said he favored one of the guys from that group. When he came here he was only supposed to have been here a couple of weeks but ended up staying months. I traveled up to Chicago to the bus station to pick him up. My cousin and partner in crime went up with me. As we waited for his bus to pull in, I was wondering which man was him. There were some fine men rolling pass me on the bus and I was so nervous about meeting him. I remember he told me a story about a girl he had traveled to Chicago to meet previously. He said that she had met him, and then told him she had to go to the restroom and then she left him at the bus station. That right there should have been my indication of what I was dealing with but NOOO! If I hadn't had such a big heart I probably would have done the same. When that bus rolled up and I saw someone staring at me, I told my cousin, "I pray that is NOT him" she agreed and then started to give me a glimpse of hope by saying that it was not. Well, guess what??? It was him. I cannot describe to you the numb feeling I felt when he walked up to me and hugged me. It is a 2 ½ hour drive from Chicago to Peoria and let me tell you, I was numb the whole ride home, it felt like it was a 5-hour drive. Every time he would touch my arm or try to talk to me, I started hearing my coworker's voices saying all those what ifs. I just knew there was no way I could ever let them meet him. I would just say he was physically challenged and leave it at that, but noooooo he paid me a surprise visit to State Farm one day and the girls got to see him live and in the flesh. I was embarrassed to say the least. This guy whom I should have left in Chicago like the other young lady did, would go on to steal $500 out of my back account, he bought me gifts with my own money, broke my glass tables, and threatened to come back to Peoria to kill me. He even made those threats to my dad. And if anyone knows anything about my Papa Bear, they know that he does not play when it comes to his children and family. I had gotten an order of protection against this guy, and I had to find a crafty way to get it to him, because every time a police officer went to serve him, he was nowhere to be found. Me being crafty and creative, I called him and pretended like I had his W2 forms and wanted to send them to him. He gave me his address and I sent him the papers to serve him. He phoned me outraged when he got the package. I remember him calling me out of my name; I mean I was everything but a child of God that day. Even though that was not a valid way of serving him the judge said it proved to them they had the correct address and they finally served him. Before he left from Peoria, I called his mom to let her know what was going on and I even got a chance to talk to his brother and I found out that this man was an ordained preacher, and he was running from God. His brother said he had a habit of lying. What a combination, a minister, and a huge liar. I found out that he did not just have a one-way ticket like he lied and said he had, but he had a round trip ticket and lied to me so that he could stay longer. His brother also told me that he had stolen money from them as well. This guy made it a point to tell me that there were many times he stood over my bed while I was sleeping contemplating on killing me and how. I thank God for his covering and protection. This guy had the audacity to send me a friend invite on Facebook... I had to decline and block him. The devil is a whole entire lie. I sure hope that this gentleman stopped running from God and that he has allowed God to use him. I do believe he is married now and pray that his marriage last until the end of time, and that they are a power couple for the kingdom. I truly do forgive this gentleman. When the devil has a stronghold on someone's life it is not them that you are up against, it is that spirit in them. I was not fully armed in the spirit to fight this devil, so God stepped in and did what I could not do and once again I came out of this mess victorious.

My daughter's father was someone I definitely set aside some of my beliefs for. I would not date anyone who was going through a divorce because they were technically still married, but I set that aside. I would never date someone who said they used to do drugs but did not anymore for fear of them relapsing, but I set that aside for him. The first sign that I should have walked away was the missing money in my purse. He even removed himself from the equation later calling me telling me he was sorry for taking my money, money that I had not realized was missing from my purse. He asked me to come see him and talk about it, and I did, and then pulling on my heartstrings and giving promises that he would never use drugs again, I forgave him and continued in

18

the relationship. There were many times he would go missing for days, then show up only for me to give him a place to lay his head, get himself back together and then return to the streets. I would leave him prayers up on the door just in case he came home so he would know that I was praying for him. It did not seem to matter, that addiction had a stronger hold on him than me and my prayers had. Still, I didn't want to walk away from someone when they were down, so I stayed. This man stole my television and sold it for drugs, sold my cell phone for drugs, pawned my car out to the drug dealers and when my daughter was just 3 days old he took all of her clothes to the drug dealer for drugs, and I had to go get money out my account to take to the dealer to get my baby's stuff back. He told me he had taken only few items from my daughter's closet, as if that was still cool and it wasn't… when the man came out the house to give me back my things, he came out with a 30-gallon garbage bag full with my baby girls belongings. Everything in her closet was in that bag. I got everything back except a dress like the one that my mom and dad bought my daughter and niece alike, they were only 3 days apart and had my parents asked us to dress them both in those outfits I would have had to come clean about what happened to the outfit. I was too embarrassed; in fact, I lied to my parents about why I had to leave their house so abruptly after having had a C-section. It was years later they would find out the real reason I really left that day in a hurry and on a mission. After he pulled this stunt I realized that I could not raise a child and run after a grown man. I gave him 9 months to get his life together and it seemed like he was getting worse. I even remember one of his buddies telling me that I was enabling him by giving him a place to stay and always being there for him when he was down. I thought I could draw him in…after all the bible declares with loving kindness have I drawn thee, but I had to learn that God also gives us the strength to walk away from situations that are harmful to our well-being and not conducive to our destiny. One thing my dad taught me is that a child needs their father, so I always left the door open for my daughter's father to have a relationship with his daughter, but I am sad to say he never took the opportunity to get to know her while she was little. He was still in his addiction and in and out of prison for robberies to feed his habit. He would write to her and promise to come see her when he got out, he would get out and those promises never came into fruition. I tried to teach my daughter to love him in spite of; that the bible teaches us to honor our father and mother as written in the Ten Commandments. It got harder over the years for her to do that when he kept breaking his promises. Before my dad transitioned from this world (whom Niyah considered her dad), he told me that I had done all I could to allow this man to have a relationship with his daughter and that I could now let it go. I did just that, I no longer made her call him back or check on him, if she did not want to talk, I did not make her do so. I just let her move at her own pace when she was ready to deal with him. Even now, he does not do all that he can. He has never given me any money to help support her. I never put him on child support because I did not want him to have any say so about her well-being or upbringing. You would think that since I did not force him to pay child support, that he would be willing to step up and help me support her, make sure she had food to eat etc.., but that was just wishful thinking. I do believe he bought her groceries 2 times over the 20 years she has been on this earth. She had to call and tell him that she needed food; even then being selfish he said he had to make sure he put groceries in his house before getting her any. I really wanted to go off on him, but I held my peace. It is hard to see your child get mistreated by the one who helped make her. His job was to provide for her, protect her, and he failed. I think out of all the forgiving this was the hardest one to do yet. He disappointed, hurt, and let down my heart and soul, my child, someone I would lay down my life for. Trying to protect her from being bitter and hurt from this situation and wanting to protect her from her first let down being from a man, I taught her to love in spite of and to know that when a person has an addiction they are not thinking properly and it isn't that he does not love her, but he can't even love himself enough to get and stay clean. I taught her the power of prayer. When he was released from prison, he stayed in contact with me for a couple of months and then vanished again. The Lord even used me to pray with him and for him. That is spiritual growth and maturity and none of this would have been possible had it not been for the love that Christ gave me and for the love that I have for Christ. It is my desire to please him and in pleasing him I must live by the fruit of the spirit, which is love, joy, peace, patience, kindness, goodness, faithfulness, and self-control.

No matter what I'm faced with, I must always represent God well in all things and at all times.

Chapter 4

Healing process

The healing process is not always easy or quick, it takes time to heal. Isn't it good to know that God is a healer, a comforter an ever-present help. I had to allow God to do the work in me. He had to help me love those who had hurt me like he loves them. It is not always easy, but it is necessary. Bitterness will keep you broken. God is a God who takes broken pieces and molds them into masterpieces. When an appliance breaks or is broken, we take it back to the manufacturer or a specialized agent for repair. We trust that if we can get the appliance to the ones who made the appliance, that they will be able to run a diagnostic test, figure out what is wrong with it and fix it. Why then do we not run to the Master when we are broken? He knew us before the world was formed. Only God can truly mold us and make us whole again. When God heals, it is a job done right. He is our warranty. God knew we would mess up but he a loving and just God. God heals hearts, minds, he heals deep wounds. No matter what it may be, if you have been a victim of rape or molestation, God is a God that can heal those deep wounds. Maybe you were abandoned by someone, God can fill that void. Maybe like me, you have been lied to and cheated on and made to feel like you were not good enough, God is a God who restores, and he is a God of inclusion. Know that you are relevant, what others did to harm you was not your fault. You are more than your past and your past cannot define who you are or where you are going. There are times the enemy will come in and make us question if we are truly healed, if our heart is able to love, if we are able to trust; we can do all things through Christ. There are times we must ask him to help us love others, and to expose or reveal to us whether someone is good for us. If we allow God to lead us through the healing process and do not allow the enemy to plant seeds of doubt, He will be able to do a work in us. We must declare and decree that we are victorious, we are loved, we are needed, we are wanted, and we will have healthy relationships where we can trust others without fear of being rejected, hurt or that the cycle will repeat itself. We must be healed for real. We cannot help others heal when we are in a hurt place.

I had to be real with myself. I spent so much time trying to please man that I was not trying to do what was pleasing to God. Although, I would like to think the Lord held first place in my life, I have to be honest and say he was not. Not like he should have been. I loved him; I knew I could depend on him; I even knew who to call in times of trouble and he would answer because he is a good father and gracious God, who always came to my aide. He did not let me stay down too long. I believe he allowed things to happen to push me closer to him, and to push me into purpose. I had to allow him to lead me in every area of my life, not just the areas I pick and choose, but I had to let the Lord have free reign over my whole entire life. There is no area he does not want to bless us in. He healed my body, he let me come back into this world for another chance to get it right and to be with my baby girl, and he delivered me out of the bondage of the enemy. He set me free from an on to the next man and not healing from the previous man mentality. He delivered me from soul ties and seeds that were planted by soul ties, fornication, watching porn, dating another man to get over the other man, and from allowing the wrong people access to my life. He delivered me being thirsty for love and a relationship and instead to thirst after him, God has delivered me and whom he sets free, is free indeed.

He never gave up on me even though at times I gave up on myself. I was good at putting on facades that people actually thought I never had any issues or problems. Part of that was due to the faith I had/have, and part was due to me not being a person to succumb to my issues and problems. I always knew that it would all work out in the end. At this point in my life, I just want to do what is pleasing in God's sight. I got tired of always giving so much of myself to others and not getting a third of it back. I no longer wanted to seek approval of others. The only approval I need is the approval of God. Spending more time with the Master and listening to him and talking to him is my desire.

I just want more of God and to be used by him. Pastor Jameliah Gooden says it best and I wear the shirt proudly, "The only man allowed to use me is Jesus".

The enemy wanted to keep me distracted back then and even more so now that I have totally submitted to God's will and his way. He was really coming for your girl; anything imaginable and anyone he could control he used. God is greater than the enemy and although at times it may seem we are losing the battle, we are actually on the winning team. With God we win! No weapon the enemy tries to use will thrive, he is cut down and consumed by fire in Jesus' name. I not only have become bold in the Lord, but he has also allowed me to become bold with the enemy...so now when someone I do not care to talk to comes up to me and ask if I miss them (the nerve right), I simply reply "no I do not." Where I would try to choose my words to deliver a soft blow, I now will give it to them with force. I have no time for sugar coating things or entertaining the enemy in this season. I rebuke all distractions in Jesus name.

Everything I have been through was to give me a testimony to encourage someone else. I do not despise the lessons I had to learn. They taught me to cling to God, his word and to align myself with his will. Stop trying to handle things on my own and allow God to direct my course. If I can go through heartbreak in relationships, disappointment on jobs, the death of my father, then I can handle love, wins and victories and I can still have joy and push through in midst of my greatest hurt. It is all because of Jesus.

The enemy will have us feeling ashamed to tell our stories and where God has brought us from, he will mask the shame while we allow him to have us living reckless lives. God comes that we might have life and life more abundantly. We overcome by our testimonies. Everyone has a past, some people are still living in theirs, but I praise God I have learned from mine.

Chapter 5

The Dream

When I was dating the guy whose ex-girlfriend vandalized my car, I had this dream. In this dream that took place in this dark room, the only light that shown threw was the crack of light that came from under the door. There were many metal cots; on each cot was a woman who had a blanket and every so often someone would get a girl and take them to the monster. Once came for, they never returned. I watched many women get taken away scared to see what was on the other side of that door. I started to notice that every time one of the blankets went from full to half (almost as though it was unraveling), the monster would send for that girl. I looked down at my blanket and saw it getting shorter and shorter, so when the monster sent for another girl, I would take their blanket and add it on to mine, giving me a full blanket. This went on and on for a while, at least until the monster caught on to the fact that my blanket would never get short, he decided he was going to come for me regardless of the length of my blanket. I was warned that he was coming, so instead of waiting for him, I decided that I would go look for him. I walked out the door and approached what looked like a kitchen with a door that led down some stairs; as I opened the door this huge snake came at me and I struggled and fought the snake by choking it, and as I was fighting this snake, I woke up. I woke up puzzled and after asking God what the dream meant, he revealed to me the meaning. The girls were all the women this man that I was dating had hurt, he would hurt them so and stripped them down to nothing. Their blankets represented their faith, their covering if you will. Once he would strip away their faith and belief system, he could devour them. By me taking their blanket and adding it to mine signified that no matter what I was facing, I did not lose my faith in God and my belief system was intact. I just kept finding more faith to get me through and as long as I had my faith to stand on, I was secure.

There are times the enemy will try to weaken our faith and our belief system, but we have to remember that God will never leave us nor forsake us. Even though we may be going through our lowest valley, we can look to the hills from whence cometh our help. 2 Corinthians 4:16-18 instructs us *"Therefore we do not lose heart. Though outwardly we are wasting away, yet inwardly we are being renewed day by day. For our light and momentary troubles are achieving for us an eternal glory that far outweighs them all. So, fix our eyes not on what is seen, but on what is unseen, since what is seen is temporary, but what is unseen is eternal."*

Chapter 6

Encounter with God

It was a couple of years after my gastric bypass (weight loss surgery); I had just left State Farm and started working at the hospital when I became very sick. I was a new mommy, and my baby was about 6 months old. I started noticing some things going on and asked a doctor about the issues. He told me that it sounded like I was bleeding somewhere in my body. This went on for a week. One morning as I was getting ready for work, I had the feeling of nausea. As I was standing in my living room, blood clots started pouring out my nose and my mouth. I had to be rushed to the hospital by my mom. While in the emergency room I got up to use the rest room and I felt myself go down. I remember lying there staring at the ceiling and the bright light; I could hear everyone around me. I heard my mother saying my name over and over; I answered, but they did not hear me for some reason. I heard the doctors say her eyes are closing, and I remember thinking these people are crazy, I am looking right up at the bright light fixture. I heard them say her pressure is dropping. After that I did not hear much; there was silence and the bright light. I laid there staring up at what I thought was the ceiling light; I remember talking to the Lord. I call to mind telling him that I cannot go yet. Lord you gave me a beautiful daughter; she is too young she needs her mother. I must be around to see her get older, go to college, get married, and have children. As I continued to lay there the noise of the ER came rushing back. I could hear them saying her blood pressure is stabilizing, she is opening her eyes. I chuckled behind that one because my eyes were open the whole time staring at the light. I heard someone say, she is smiling. When I woke up in ICU I asked my mom what was wrong with them. I heard you calling my name, but you did not answer. I heard them say my eyes were closed and my eyes were open the whole time staring at the light. That is when my mom told me that my eyes were not open and that they had lost me and then

I came back. That is when I realized that my bright light moment was an encounter with God. I do not remember him saying anything, although it felt like an exchange of dialogue; I remember him just listening and then he answered my heart. Just thinking about this makes me emotional. What an awesome God to grant a wish of someone who was not aware they were gone. To allow me to have added years because he loves me is so overwhelming. The enemy tried to take me out a couple of more times, but God said not so. How can I not serve a God like this? My baby is now 20 years old and we are truly enjoying each other. God has a work for both of us to do.

Chapter 7

Compassion…a Gift or a Curse

How can two walk together except they agree? This does not mean to agree with your choice of movie or agree on where to go eat, but it means to agree in spirit. The spiritual aspect of agreeing I tried to ignore when it came to most of the men I dated. Instead of waiting on the Lord, I allowed myself to be entertained by people I knew were close to being the devil's spawn.

One of the gifts God gave me is compassion, and with this gift if not used wisely with discernment, it will cause you to look at a person who is telling you who they are, which may be a liar, a womanizer, a drug abuser, and alcoholic, a dead beat dad, a person who uses profanity and does not know how to hold an intelligent conversation, a user who wants money or sex and sometimes both, a thief, the list could go on for days but compassion can have you finding the one thing in that person that is good and make them out to be better than they are instead of taking them at face value. It can make self-feel foolish. Take for instance when I dated a guy that was Muslim (not nation of Islam, but I dated that type too…whew) from a spiritual aspect, we had no business being together. I thought the love we had for each other would conquer all. The friendship aspect of him was pretty dope as long as we did not talk about religion; some of the heated discussions we got in should have been an indicator to run, but if I am being completely honest, the sex was a homerun every time so that made it a lot harder to leave. I had to learn the hard way which involved major crushing and heartache, and by the time I decided to get out of the relationship, there was a deep soul tie that would take years to break. Soul ties are real, and they attach you to a person in spirit even if you are not with that person in the physical. They can also hold you up in the spirit from meeting the person God has chosen for you to have. So, when God gives us warning like he did in 2 Corinthians 6:14 "Be ye not unequally yoked together with unbelievers: for what fellowship hath righteousness with unrighteousness? And what communion hath light with darkness? He meant it for our good, not as a punishment but warning before destruction. He knew the amount of warfare this type of union could bring. Since he is a great father he will try to protect us, and we have to be obedient or face the consequences.

Sometimes we can give people too much of ourselves and we begin to morph into someone different; someone who God did not intend for us to be. We can be loving and caring but we do not need to bend or change the way we are to appease a person. If we do that and it is not a change that we feel we need to make for growth and that we are being forced to make, it can cause resentment and we can lose ourselves. The person God has for you will not need you to change and he or she will welcome every aspect of you. They will not run from but embrace you, pray with and for you and love you unconditionally. They will not just take from you and drain you, but a true relationship be it friendship or romantic is built on trust and reciprocation. Moreover, they will not steer you away from God, but they will push you further into purpose.

Christ is love and because Christ made us we should not change our DNA in the Lord to mesh with the DNA of the world.

Chapter 8

Unequally Yoked

My experience with Mr. Unequally Yoked gets a chapter all its own. When I met Mr. Unequally Yoked, I was very taken aback at how handsome and educated he was. He was a nice height, smooth dark complexion, drove and had his own car, he talked with much intellect, and like most women, I love a man with beautiful teeth and a pretty smile. His smile could light up a room. His teeth were white, he had nicely chiseled arms and his physique was that of an athlete… what did this man want with me? I had met a few men here and there over the years by way of internet. It was the new thing to do then, and everyone was doing it, so those I did not meet in passing, I met online. My parents were not thrilled by this method of meeting people but gone were the days of going out and meeting people especially if you were like me, always sat in the house. I had to explain to them that this was the new thing. Some of the guys I met were a little challenged in the physical realm which also matched with their personality. So, when I met Mr. Unequally Yoked, to say I was smitten by him would be an understatement. I met him on BlackPlanet. Yeah I know I just dated myself again, but I'm sticking with my story of being 22 and holding LOL. BlackPlanet was a platform for people to meet and network. I am not sure if anyone uses it anymore these days. I talked with Mr. Unequally Yoked for a while and then he came down from school to visit me. His school was about an hour and thirty minutes away. During the course of our relationship, I would find myself and my daughter traveling many nights sometimes at midnight just to be with this man. He did the same so I did not feel like it was always on me, we both put some miles on our cars and if I am going to be honest, not all with Mr. Unequally Yoked was bad; however, the bad should have made me walk away, but I stayed four years too long. At first

31

he came off like a charmer and he spoke a great game. Having a child and her father not being involved in her life was hard for me especially since my father had always been a part of my life; so, when I met Mr. Unequally Yoked and he talked about his children and how much they meant to him, that pulled at my heartstrings. The issues he was having with his children mothers should have been a red flag but I wanted to believe him and his side of the story so I shut out what their truth was and sided with him for a while that is, until I got to see firsthand that even though he talked a good game and tried, he could have done better.

I can't tell you that there were no red flags, and I will not tell you that I didn't ignore some of them, because I did. When I met Mr. Unequally Yoked it was some time after my weight loss surgery. In fact when I met him, I was over 100 pounds down from my original weight. I remember this man lying on my couch while I was sitting in a chair, we were talking and out of nowhere he says "how does it feel to be the biggest person in your family? Your mom and your sisters are little, but you are the only big person... how does that make you feel?" I remember asking him how it felt to be the biggest butthole in his family...and I did not say it that nicely either. The more he kept talking to me, I felt like I was being taunted all over again by grade school kids. I never thought in my adult life that I would have to face the demons of my childhood and by someone I was dating and sleeping with. In my mind I was wondering if it was such a problem then why was he driving miles upon miles to spend time with me, yet he wants to talk about me... I never understood it and although I was hurt by it, I continued to deal with him. He would always throw up in my face that I was a Christian and he was Muslim and Christians were hypocrites, this he did mostly when we were arguing. For the most part I did not think of our different religions as an issue as long as he respected my view and I respected his, even if I didn't agree with the way he thought. I respected him as a person and if I were to love him, I would truly love him, differences and all. After the taunting of my weight and it happened on more than one occasion... he was good at hurting my feelings, then apologizing and being on good behavior for a while, just to let me down again. I would go on to lose over 78

32

more pounds. I did it mostly out of revenge, satisfying my desire by thinking when I lose all this weight; I am going to leave him in the rear-view mirror. That however was not the case. I got down to a size 14 and I stayed with him. Then it was an issue of my having lost too much weight because he liked the fuller face. I tell you if it wasn't one thing it was another. I started to open my eyes and see that all the women in his past and present were not little women. They all had weight on them. Then why was it a problem for me to have some on me? Thinking back on it now, God revealed to me that even though I was losing weight in the natural, I was allowing myself to be weighted down spiritually by being with that man, which is probably why after the relationship was over, a huge weight lifted off of me.

Mr. Unequally Yoked was the kind of man who would say we were together as a couple, and then he would say he was single when he wanted to step outside of the relationship, or he may have already done so. I remember countless times he had introduced me to people that he had slept with. No! I was not aware of it at the time he would introduce me, but I started to put some things together later. I recall being on the elevator with a female in his building, she was giving me dirty looks, only for me to find out later that he had slept with her a few days before…when I found out about it and called him out on it, he told me the details even more than I cared to hear and how she wore my same fragrance of perfume. That was it for me right?? Wrong, I still stayed with him! I once found movie tickets on his dresser while helping him clean. When I questioned him about it, he lied at first then after some grilling about it and making him feel bad, he came clean and told me that the day he said he was going out with the boys he took a lady from Africa to the movies. This was one of the many ladies I knew about, or I should say one of the many ladies I coaxed him into coming clean about. This is the first time I am revealing this, but I had his password to his phone. There were many nights I intercepted phone calls and text messages from women, who were telling him how they loved him and how good he made them feel in bed and how they could not wait to talk to him and see him again. Side note people, if you have to do all this to get a man/woman or keep them, they are not worth keeping. Get you a peace of mind by letting him or her go. Nevertheless, it took me a while to get to the point of letting go. One young lady that I remember was a female that had stayed the weekend with him at his apartment, mind you the apartment I helped him clean up, just so another woman could stay there. The story I got from him was that he was going to Iowa to stay over at a buddy's house who had graduated from his school already. I was cool with that because my pastor was having a dinner for our church so it just worked out that I could not hang with him anyway. I received an occasional text from him while he was "with his buddy." He called once, we did not talk long, but we spoke so I felt secure that he was where he said he was to be. Later after my church event when he did not answer the phone, I didn't feel too bothered by it, I just figured the guys were having fun… oh but that Monday, when I decided to listen to his voicemail I heard a young lady telling him that she had made it home and she enjoyed the weekend they spent together… oh you best believe I called her to make my presence known and I interrogatingly made him tell me the truth about it after him trying to lie…oh but I did not divulge the secret that I had his pass code…nope a lady never tells. I felt like a football team member, I was making all kinds of interceptions. I remember making up songs and adding the name of the girl who had tried to leave him a voice message. I would sing it while we were sitting on the couch watching movies. He was never the wiser or maybe he just didn't care.

There are times I question why I allowed myself to be subjected to such hurt and pain and if I am being honest, to mental abuse? I was there for this man when he needed support. I would spend holidays with his family in his hometown and not spend them with my family. Super bowls that I would have watched with my dad I spent with him. When this man was sick, I would get on the road with my 6-year-old; nurse him back to health only to get back on the road at 4am to get back in town for work and to get my daughter off to school. None of this was good enough for him. I often heard him say, "You are a good woman, but it may be someone better out there". He would say this when he was seeing someone else on the side. I knew in my heart that this was not a relationship that God wanted me in. His purpose was served when he reached out to the school I was interested in attending to get my bachelor's degree. He gave them my information for them to contact me. I thought it was divine intervention, but it was God using Mr. Unequally Yoked to make a move when I was procrastinating. I will forever be grateful that he took the initiative and contacted the school that I was interested in. Because of that email he sent on my behalf, I not only got my bachelor's, but received my master's degree as well. So, while some may look at me sideways for staying with him, something good came out of this rollercoaster ride.

The final straw was when I was dealing with my dad being sick and I was strolling through Facebook and saw a picture that he was tagged in where he had gone to a wedding with another girl. Mind you I could hardly ever get him to go to a family function especially after him and my family had a falling out. But I asked him to go to a wedding with me, it was a close coworkers wedding and this man told me he did not want to go, but yet he went to a wedding with this young lady and to top it all off, on valentine's day he stood me up to be with her and out of that union they had a child. It may puzzle some as to why this young lady was the end all be all to me putting up with this man's mess, but she really wasn't. It was something deeper and for the sake of everyone involved, let me just say this… I could not honor my dad's name and be with this man. I know that what happened between this man and I was something that had to happen because God knew his unfaithfulness was not going to make me leave him. God knew that the level of lowness that this man stooped to and what he said that day, would send me packing.

If there was anything that I can take away from this relationship, it was that I learned to love myself more…it is ok to love others but when it affects your self-esteem and value, then it is time to let it go and love yourself more than you love that person.

It is not ok to deal with verbal or mental abuse. I realize now that nothing I could have done would have ever been enough for this man to love me the way I deserved to be loved.

If you think this was the end to the story you could not be more wrong. Mr. Unequally Yoked later moved to another state to be with another young lady and I was the one he called when this young lady broke his heart. I had to comfort the one person who hurt me to my core several times. It would have been so easy to laugh at him and tell him he was getting what he deserved but I did not. I was there for him as a friend only, nothing more and I gave him some really solid advice that helped him move on.

What I went through was not by mistake. God chose me to go through it so that I could encourage others and let them know that our tragic past is not our final destination. God can and will use everything that the enemy thought would take us out, for his glory. So often we ask God why me, and God is saying you are the why! I made you to be a witness and a living testimony that no matter what life may throw your way, you can do all things through me!

Chapter 9

Fed Up

After dealing with the guy who was involved with the Nation of Islam, I took a little break before dating anyone else. I had decided to just be alone, and I became fine with not dealing with anyone. I would always post scriptures on Facebook; it was my way of spreading good news and cheer to all who may have been in need of a pick me up. I received a friend request from a guy and when I checked his page, he looked like a nice handsome working single father. Single parent stood out heavily because I have always been a single mom. It was comforting to see a father stepping up taking responsibility and raising his child. So, I accepted his friend request. Thinking nothing of it, I would engage in a conversation with him every now and again, but it was nothing that I felt was flirtatious or promising; I was just being a witness for the Lord, answering questions that were asked and trying to help him understand the word better. Unbeknownst to me he had other motives, and he used my relationship with God as bait. He asked me out and we met at a restaurant, he was quite the gentleman. We talked about God and our children, about failed relationships and the things we learned from them and what we would and would not tolerate in a relationship going forward. As we sat there eating and talking and enjoying each other's company, he asked if he could take me to the movies and I agreed. Of course, I had to text my girls and my daughter to let them know things were going well. He was showing all the signs of being a person who would be ideal to date. After our initial date we spoke for a few days on the phone then he asked if he could stop by. Feeling comfortable enough with him, I decided to let him come over. He brought his daughter over to visit as well. I noticed that he bought a lot of her things over as well (toys, clothes, hair items etc.). She was very spirited and a cutie. My baby girl told me she was not sure she could get along with this little girl, but she would try. I had to remind Niy that not everyone was raised the way she was, and you cannot smother a child's spirit, but you can guide them. That day he brought his daughter over, I found myself doing her hair and getting her ready for bed so he would not have to do it once they went home. He came, dropped her off and said he would be back…he never came back until the next morning. Little did he know that his daughter gave my daughter the tea about what was going on in their home life. She told my daughter that she liked me better than her dad's girlfriend (of which I knew nothing about) because she was mean, and she hoped things would work out with us because she really liked the both of us. During the course of him being gone we called him and he told us he was bringing dinner, several hours later and knowing these kids had to get up for school I decided to cook dinner and it was a good thing I did, because he never came back that night…he called and gave me a lame excuse about still having to take care of some things in his storage unit and as soon as it was straightened out, he would be along. The next morning as I was getting the girls ready for school he showed up; this was around 6:30 am. He came dressed for work acting like he did not just leave his little girl at a stranger's house all night. Not being one who likes to argue I looked at him and told him I have been here before sir, and this feeling is oh too familiar and one I do not want to relive. If this is who he is, a person who lies and does not keep his word, I do not want to continue our friendship. He assured me that he was not trying to play games, and that he was sorry and the night that he did not come back and get his daughter, he got into it with his ex and rather than bring those negative vibes around me he just stayed away… I could see right through his lame story. I had no time to even dwell on it; I had to get my baby to school and myself to work.

That evening he came back but he had taken his daughter over her grandmother's house. The vibes that he was giving off were strange to say the least I felt like he was imposing himself into my home and life, and it started to feel too familiar as if I had been there done that. I also started noticing that every time he came over he would bring a few things and leave them at my home!

One day while we were hanging out I decided to run a few errands and he asked if he could tag along. He asked if we could run by his place for something, he would not tell me what he was doing, he also asked me if I would not mind driving so he could leave his car at my house, again I thought this request was strange. As we are circling his apartment building I start questioning why he was not going in, he would just say I'm trying to see something…then he gets out puts his keys in an empty mailbox. I again question why he put his keys in the mailbox for anyone to come along and get them. He said because his ex was going to come get them; she needed to get something from HIS apartment. None of this made sense to me. I remember seeing an angry young lady walking towards the mailbox. She passed my car, looked but kept walking. God let me know at that moment what time it was. That was his girlfriend his daughter told me and my daughter about, and they were breaking up and the apartment that was supposedly HIS was HERS and he was homeless. When we got back to my house I watched this man drink a whole bottle of alcohol. Not a small bottle but it was a tall bottle and since I am not a drinker I cannot tell you the exact size, but it was not the size for a person who said they would occasionally have a drink on the weekend from time to time. It was the size of a person who was a seasoned drinker (an alcoholic). I really started paying attention and tying it all together. He left for a while and later returned to my house smelling like a dead skunk. He had been out smoking weed. This man drank, this man smoked, this man lies…he was at 3 strikes and as they say in baseball, YOU'RE OUT!!! I am a believer that God being God will use whom he wishes to use, to get an assignment done…I remember praying to God to remove this man from my life if I was not to be connected to him in any way. As I was sitting at work the next day, I started receiving text messages about being a cheater. Mind you I have not committed to this guy I was trying to be friendly and help someone out, but now I am a cheater. I didn't know what he was talking about, but I was like… Ok let's roll with it. I engaged in the conversation for a while and told him I had to get back to work. After work I got a call from him asking me if we could talk. I agreed. He started driving stating that I was going to a club to watch him play cards…I told him I was not going to no club and that if he wanted to talk, then talk! This man was raising his voice at me talking about how I had people calling me because I was still dating them and that he does not play games. Then it dawned on me that he was referring to a phone call that I had received the previous day. You know I had to go in on him and tell him about himself. I had to remind him that he was not my man and that he took me out to his apartment complex and dragged me into some mess unknowingly. As small as Peoria is he could have had this girl looking for me for absolutely no reason at all. I told him that I would not be yelled at as if I am a child and to take me home this conversation was over. Later that night he called asking for a blanket, he stated he was homeless and had to sleep in his car. I asked where his daughter was he told me not to worry about it and insisted on having me give him a blanket. I told him no he could not have a blanket and to have a great night. I remember him texting me "thank you I am going to freeze because of you." Once I figured out his little girl was not with him and she was safe, it was no longer my problem where he slept. I do know that he was trying to make me feel bad for his bad choices and decisions, but I was not falling for it. As I laid in bed that night I was like whew my Lord how did things change overnight. Then I recalled the prayer I prayed to the Lord. It was then I realized that God is a right now God. He answered my prayers right after I prayed to him.

Two days later I got a call from the imposer asking me to pack up all his stuff and he would pick it up. I questioned what stuff he had here other than his daughter's toys and hair stuff and this should only take a quick moment. I told him once I gathered it I would call him to come get it. When I tell you I had not realized this guy had brought so much into my house, it was a whole 30-gallon garbage bag full of stuff and then some stuff still did not fit in the bag. I was floored at how this guy was really trying to make my house his home on the sly. Old devil! The devil will sneak in on the prowl looking for someone to devour. He will disguise himself as someone totally different to gain access into places he is not allowed. He walked into my house with an attitude and did not say a word to me or my daughter. Then I went to the door asked him where his daughter was (Oce love the kids) and he signaled for me to hold on, hopped in the car and pulled off fast. All I could do I laugh at him and praise God in the same breath.

One of the hardest things to do but is instructed by the Lord is to bless those who curse you, and to pray for those who mistreat you. This man treated me as if I had done something to him. He blocked me on Facebook (boo-hoo) which was not a big deal I just happened upon something to know that he blocked me I surely did not try to access his page to see. It puzzled me for a moment how someone could change so quickly towards you in the speed of light. I then started to think back to the days prior when I asked the Lord that if this man was not to be connected to me, end it right now. Let me tell you, God will give you what you ask for. I had gotten so used to asking God to remove people who were not supposed to be connected to me and knowing he would do it, but with this guy I really felt a totally different connection at first, so I hadn't even thought to have that talk with the Lord about him, but when I did, he removed him and right away. I learned that you cannot pick and choose where to insert God into a situation. You should always go to him first and do not shy away from what he does or what he tells you. I am here to tell someone that when you ask something of the Lord and you believe he will do it, expect it to happen. God is not playing around in this season. He will not allow his children to continually be hurt or subjected to that which will cause them harm. So, I had to get out of my feelings about how this guy walked away so abruptly and realize that it was an answered prayer. Had it ended amicably it would have afforded him some type of access to me. I would have become more attached to his daughter, who was my main concern, and I would have probably been sucked in. I thank God for knowing how and when to end things. It may not feel good, but it is necessary. The pain was necessary…it was then I had a talk with the Lord.

I decided to give God a complete yes. I saw how he began to turn things around for me. I decided to wait on God to bring the right person to me. I knew that whatever God wanted me to do; I wanted to be busy doing it.

I was on a Facebook live, I don't even know how I happened upon it, if someone tagged me or invited me or shared the live, I do not remember to this day, but I do remember the host calling out my name and letting me know that God said I was to be in her mentoring class and that there was something she was to impart in me… This young lady was to serve as my spiritual mid-wife and help pull something out of me that God needed brought out, for me to go forward in him. The day I found out I was a prophetic intercessor was the day

41

that everything I had always done concerning my prayer life made sense to me. How I knew what to pray and how to pray for people without them telling me what they needed and why I could not flip through Facebook and pretend I did not see someone ask for prayer and not pray for them. I would try to scroll by it real fast but Holy Spirit would check me instantly and I would have to go back and pray.

When you think the devil has had the last say God will give you the last laugh. While I think that the way the imposer departed could have been handled better and no doubt he thought he really did something big by pulling off down the street all fast, that was not that last I heard of him. He called about 6 months later asking if he could take me to lunch. I told him I was not interested; I forgive him, no lunch was needed, and that I respectfully decline. I told him to have a great life and take care of that beautiful little girl. I am guessing that didn't set well with him because he texted me saying that it must feel good to respectfully decline…I just laughed, blocked his number, and thanked my Lord and savior for helping me dodge a bullet.

Chapter 10

The Surrender

The enemy fought me so hard because he knew the assignment that God had for me. That old devil will have you questioning and second guessing what it is that God really wants you to do. Can I write it, who am I to tell it, nobody will listen, I will be judged, but we should know that it is a trick of the enemy to stop us from pushing forward and finishing what God has put in us. He will cause you to question your authority to speak on different subjects. How can I speak on trust when I have been hurt? How can I tell someone to never give up on love when I have been deceived by it? God!!! is how... Jesus' exemplary display of love and forgiveness is the reason I can forgive and love and pray for my enemies.

Jesus is breaking chains and delivering his children. It is not his will for us to be enslaved to our past or our beliefs, but to have faith in him and trust his word.

Looking back on all that I have encountered in my life I can honestly say God was with me. I now can look back and appreciate all the lessons that life taught me. Often we feel that a no, or not now, or being looked over for promotions or failed relationships are punishments from God, but to me I see a blessing in it all. There are times when God must hide you to protect you from those who would want to pimp the gift you have. Not everyone will see or notice the gifts God put in you, but the right people will come along to make sure those gifts are brought out and put into action. Likewise, there are some who will see the gift in you and get jealous of what God had put in you that they will mishandle you and drop you, but God will replace those people with people willing to do his will and get it done. The word says that all things are working for me. That does not mean I get the things I want all the time, but that lets me know, whether a yes or no, God is constantly working on my behalf. That car that did not start right away one morning, that promotion you may have gotten overlooked for, that man or woman you may have pruned for another person, whatever it may be, do not look at it as whoa it's me, but approach it from a thankful stance. Thank you Lord that the car did not start, you may have avoided a huge car pile up, thank you father that I didn't get stuck in that dead end stressful job, thank you that I no longer have that headache of a man or woman that was depleting all my time and energy.

God does not make mistakes if something did not happen the way you intended it to, that is ok. It is Gods will that will prevail. He said it in his word that many are the plans in a person's heart, but it is the Lord's purpose that will prevail. I heard a preacher say, "that my betrayal brought my purpose". It is because of the betrayal that God birthed this book. A ministry came about to encourage others out of my betrayal. It is because of the betrayal that I can truly forgive and be happy. It is because of the betrayal that I held on even more tightly to the Lord.

When I finally surrendered to God and accepted that God designed me with purpose in mind, that is when I started to put all the pieces of this messed up puzzle together.

I challenge you to surrender to God and watch him turn all the mess, lies, betrayal, and hurt in your life, past or present, into a beautiful masterpiece.

There is a brand of spaghetti sauce, Prego who coined the phrase "it's in there", which was basically letting all who would purchase this brand of sauce know that all the desired ingredients that they were looking for a sauce to have, was in theirs. The same holds true for our heavenly father. If you are looking for joy, peace, love, forgiveness, deliverance, healing, happiness, restoration, and protection, direction, clarity, confidence…whatever you may need from the Holy Trinity is in there… Where is there? There is in the will and the word of God. To know the will of God will require you to get in the word of God. Our heavenly father knows best. We need only trust him, obey his will, and surrender all of our secrets that our clothes could tell over to him and he will make all things brand new.

Chapter 11

The counterfeit

Let me dispel that when you give God a yes all things go well or fall into place. Remember that there is still an enemy called the devil and he knows the plans God has for you and the impact you will make on the world, and he knows the things God wants to give you and do for you in your life.

Minding my own business and being about my Heavenly Father's business did not stop the enemy from trying to creep into my life. I remember being prophesied to that I would be getting married. I laughed because all my life I had wanted what my parents had, a strong healthy marriage, but in my humanity and all the let downs I had experienced throughout the years, I had gotten comfortable being on my own. I loved not answering to anyone, and being alone to read my word, I love lying in bed watching TV, I finally was alone and loving every minute of it. Singleness was no longer a curse to me but a beautiful thing. Then God sent a word through a prophet that He was getting ready to send me my husband that I would encounter 2 counterfeits and then the one I was to marry would come along.

Well, it happened, but the devil was so cunning that I thought I had encountered my counterfeits already that when my ex-fiancé came along I thought he was the real deal. He was real, a real pretender. He went to church; he had an active role in his church. He "seemed" to really be sold out for the Lord. He had a bible on his kitchen table that I never saw him open. Matter of fact I never saw him pray except for when I would pray over the food we would eat.

Remember when I said that I try to find the blessing in things that others would probably see as a bad thing? Covid turned out to be not such a bad thing in the sense that when covid hit, it forced me to pay attention to all that was going on around me. Churches were closed and when my church went online I started watching via Facebook live. He watched his church service a couple of times as well but only a couple of times. This man started to complain about everything (mainly because he did not stay connected to the power source which is the word of God). I was starting to see why a few people close to me that knew him before I did, did not care too much for him. They warned me to watch out for him because he was not always a truthful person.

This man would share with me about his past and his relationships and how he was the one that got done wrong. How he had adopted his ex's children and I thought that was so noble of him. For a man to adopt, love and care for children whose fathers were not present was just awesome to me. I felt he could be someone positive for my daughter to have around. Boy was I wrong.

I fell in love with his daughter and to this day we stay in touch. Even though her dad and I did not work out, my love for her was very genuine and I still love her deeply as if she were my own daughter. The way he treated his adopted boys who are her brothers did not set well with me. I watched this man who pretended to be so loving and kind, display evilness towards those boys. It broke my heart. My first time meeting his oldest son when he came to his house, I found myself having to be the peace in the home that night. He did not invite his son or his girlfriend to sit down, I had to do that. I had to tell his son how proud I was of him for keeping his job, and for acknowledging that when he met his girlfriend his perspective on life changed. I affirmed to him that the right person can change our lives for the better. I witnessed his son apologize for things he had done to him in the past and I also witnessed a father reject the apology from his son. That was the moment things changed for me. If you cannot love your kids, you must be pretending to love me and my child.

I'm not one of those mothers that will put a man before her child. In fact, I think it's important to get your child's view on things. When my daughter told me that she felt his feelings towards her had changed and she did not think that he liked her, I started to make my exit then. When I needed him to do something that would have benefited my baby and he did not, I knew then he was not the one for me. I prayed to God and I asked him to remove him if he was indeed the counterfeit and the next day, hear me and hear me well the next day that man called me and told me it was obvious I did not like him and he wanted his ring back, I gave it back to him Scorpio style. I cut open the teddy bear he gave me, and I put the ring, the band and both boxes in the bear. Before he came over to retrieve those items, he was being a butt...straight stank attitude, so I did what I thought was best for me to do. Although petty, it made me feel like I was getting him back for his attitude that I had dealt with for months. Before this point, he tried to make a few males from his family think that I was sweating him. Anyone who knows me knows that I do not chase a man. As a matter of fact, I have had several exes through the years tell me that when I say I'm done and cut someone off it's as if I never knew them. That's true to some extent, just ask my daughter's father about that. As previously mentioned, I gave him 9 months to get his stuff /life together and he did not. I guess he thought I was playing because when my daughter came I was done. I was only going to raise one child.

This man was telling his uncle and brother that I was sweating him, and baaaby if my clothes could talk they would have cursed that man out and laid all his secrets bare. If I am going to sweat a man he must first have something to sweat and worth holding on to. He just wasn't the one for me and I understood that. I understood that he had an assignment to carry out and I had a test to pass.

I felt such a peace when that relationship was over. I blocked that man on every social media platform and on my phone and I never looked back. I just thanked God for exposing the counterfeit. My prayer for you all is that he will do that same for you. That any snake no matter the age, sex, or relation to you, that God will reveal their heart and true intent. Anyone who feels stuck will begin to move forward in life and purpose once they learn to let go.

If our clothes could talk and tell all of our deepest darkest secrets what would yours tell about you? Would it tell a story of defeat, or would they tell a story of triumph and how you overcame obstacles that were sent to kill you... I am betting on the later. You are an overcomer. You are victorious and most importantly you are a child of God and of royal priesthood. Walk in it and never let anyone dim your light.

My surrendering to God allowed me to recognize the counterfeit and to move on from him with no hesitation; I knew that what God had for me was far greater than what the enemy sent. I stand on the word, promises of the Lord, and know that if he said it, it shall come to pass.

Chapter 12

The Promises

I just want to encourage someone today that when God makes a promise he keeps his word, for the Lord says it in Jeremiah 1:12 I am watching over my word to fulfill it. Life has a way of wreaking havoc, and it will have you doubting what the Lord said to you directly or a word he gave to you through one of his great prophets. Sometimes the words that he gives you is not a word for right now, but it is a word for the future and because we don't see that word manifest we get discouraged thinking that it will never happen or it's too late to happen. If God said that you will be married then you will be married. It does not matter how many years you have been single; singleness is not your portion. Wait On God and trust him. God will give you the desires of your heart. He knows better than we do what we need because he is the maker and the creator of it all. If God said that your body would be healed and the enemy keeps fighting you in that area and every time you go to the doctors there is a bad report you have to stand on the word of God that says by his stripes you are healed and that many are the afflictions of the righteous but the Lord delivers him out of them all.

God promised me that I would be married and that he has a husband for me, and I believe him, so I am willing to wait on him to send that person to me. I am at the point in my life that I want the things that God has for me because the things that God has for me is for me and they are good.

God promised me that he would bless me as far as I could see, so my prayer was that God would remove the blinders from my natural eyes and my spiritual eyes that I would be able to see things bigger and through his lenses. The word tells me that God is able to do exceedingly abundantly above all that we could ask or think. That Tells me that I serve a big God and I must think big.

I stand on the promises of God that I will not always struggle and that it is not his will for me to live paycheck to paycheck because He said, I am the lender and not the borrower, I am the head and not the tail, I am above and not beneath. The Bible tells us in Jeremiah 29:11 *for I know the plans I have for you declares the Lord plans to prosper you and not to harm you plans to give you hope and a future.* If God says that his plans are to prosper us then that means in every area of our lives whether it be spiritual prosperity, financial prosperity, mental prosperity, relational prosperity, or whatever area in your life that you desire God to prosper you in. He's a good father and he wants to bless all of our works, but don't just take my word for it; let's see what God says about it… Deuteronomy 28:12 tells us that *the Lord shall Open unto thee His good treasure, the heaven to give the rain unto thy land in his season, and to bless all the work of thine hand; and thou shalt lend unto many nations, and thou shalt not borrow.*

Whatever God has told you would happen in your life do not get discouraged if it has not happened yet, it will, trust God and trust God's timing. You will get that degree, you will have that husband or wife, you will open that business, you will have a child, you will own that dream home, you will have an integral ministry, you will write those books, you will have several streams of income, your children will be saved, and you will have favor with men, generational curses will be broken, you will be successful in life. How do you obtain those things? The answer is found in Matthew 6:33 *seek first the Kingdom of God and his righteousness, and all these things shall be added to you.* When you seek God and put Him first, He will direct you. Things will fall into place. No good thing will He withhold from you. He's a promise keeper.

God's word will manifest in your life and every promise that he has given to you will be fulfilled. Remember God loves us, we are his children, and his promises are our inheritance.

Early on in this journey the secrets that my clothes could tell were those of hurt, disappointment, discouragement, abandonment, defeat, self-sabotage, mistreatment, feeling unworthy, outright embarrassment, but now my clothes tell a different story. The story they now tell is a story of a prayer warrior who is walking in victory. I know who I am and whose I am. I'm optimistic, obedient to God, I love who I am and who I am becoming. I'm accepted, cherished, loved! I don't need to fit in because God made me to stand out. They would tell you that I am bold in the Lord and sold out for him, and my desire is to please God and be pleasing in his sight.

www.ingramcontent.com/pod-product-compliance
Lightning Source LLC
Chambersburg PA
CBHW060356130626
46553CB00003B/1256